~ || ~

WHAT ABOUT CONRAD?

Yevette Fisher

Copyright © 2020
By Globe Shakers, LLC

This book or parts thereof may not be reproduced in any form, stored in a retrieval system, or transmitted in any form; electronic, mechanical, photocopy, recording, or otherwise is not permitted without prior written permission of the authors.

ISBN 978-0-9997545-9-7
©2020
All rights reserved

Printed in the United States of America

Names have been changed to use discretion

Online store/contact info
www.globeshakers.com

Author's Other Books

Devil Let My Baby Go

Walk by Faith Prayer Journal

Momma's Last Breath

Shop online @ globeshakers.com
Covenant Gear Christian Apparel
& Prayer Pillows

Table of Contents

Foreword 2
A New Career 6
Crossing Paths ………........12
Our Bond 16
An Invitation 32
Divine Appointment 40
Reunited ….......................54
Faith flight 60
The Plan 64
God's Grace 72
Unspoken Confession 86
What About Conrad 90

Foreword

This is a great story about a beautiful friendship between my mother and a dear friend. As a young girl, I remember Conrad and by the time I was in high school he passed away. Many do not take heed to the word of God while "alive and well," but the Lord's mercy endureth forever (Psalm 136:1). I enjoyed reading this story, and it touched my heart. The book was a mixture of humor and sadness, but the ending is so joyous!

Evangelist & Author
Nichol Collins
Globeshakers.com

The author never fails to draw my attention as I have read her previous books including this most recent publication. I am in awe at the depth of love that Jesus extends to reach out to souls. This book is a Holy Ghost inspired read indeed. I felt emotions of sadness as I cried real tears. Then, I was met with praise and rejoicing towards the close of the testimony. This is a captivating story that you will not be able to put down. All glory be to God.

Renea Owens
Acts 2:38 Missionary

In this book, Evangelist Waters' question, What About Conrad? is a living demonstration of what Apostle Paul wrote regarding the heart of God in 1 Timothy 2:4; "Who will have all men to be saved, and to come unto the knowledge of the truth." This story of evangelism is a must-read for all Christians to encourage them to walk in faith and share the Good News of the Gospel to everyone within their circle. Seldom do you have the opportunity to read about a relationship that displays such genuine love and concern toward the eternal destination of a friend's soul.

Evangelist & Author
Karolyn Kellum

A New Career

When I was thirteen, I met a young man walking past my house nicknamed "Skip." I thought he was so fine. Who would have known that this connection would be my introduction to sex at the age of thirteen? The relationship became very abusive early on at about the age of fifteen. We dated all throughout senior high. Most of the time, Skip and I argued and fought like two juveniles.

We moved in together after I graduated, and our toxic soul tie continued. I endured years of domestic violence and emotional scarring. Skip was a drug dealer but had such a high IQ he could have landed in a great occupation. He later started using a drug called PCP (embalming fluid) and displaying bizarre behaviors. After giving birth to a baby girl, I decided when she was two months old that I did not want to raise her in that hostile environment.

I was twenty-two years old and at my wit's end. I abandoned my belongings to escape the abuse. I drove off with only what could fit in my car. I moved home with my mother to get a fresh start. My family was very supportive helping me with my daughter Nichol.

My cousin Bernadette put in a good word at her job on my behalf and I got hired. It was a blessing to have an opportunity for a "good government job," as my Father called it. I had the determination to provide for my baby without her dad's help. I began a new career as a reservation sales agent at Amtrak in Los Angeles, California.

My co-workers in training class were like an extended family toward one another. Our workstation was a cubicle seating at a computer. It was common to become friends with coworkers that sat around your workspace. One of them was a man named Jack that kept flirting with me, but he wasn't really my type.

The two-month training was very intense. Once completed, it was a relief to learn whether you passed the class and if so, then be notified of your start date or dismissal. A supervisor would tap you on your shoulder for a brief meeting to relay the good or bad news. Some did not make the cut. We were excited once we were promoted out of the class and had been given the chance to make some "real" money. We thought we had arrived!

Then, the big day came for all fifteen members of our class to answer the incoming calls. We were like fresh fish out of water. I was nervous about working on the main floor. This is where the rubber met the road; either you swam or sank. Nothing could compare to learning the job hands-on.

Amtrak was considered a business that offered a great opportunity for advancement. Our job description consisted of answering calls, giving information about train schedules, and booking reservations. Upon our arrival at work, we had to retrieve our headset, work files, and a notebook, which were kept in our lockers. There were many departments that you could transfer to, including the actual train station.

Our department was open twenty-four hours. It would be a while before we racked up enough seniority to leave the reservation office position. Your hire date was particularly important because it was your seniority date which determined the order in which bids you were interested in were awarded, including your off days. Yep! It was all about seniority at the reservation office and any other clerical positions in the various departments.

The management assigned all the new trainees to work in the same area for a few weeks. At the time, me, Alma, and Lilli were like the 3 Musketeers. We were all in our early twenties just young and silly. We felt intimidated by the veteran employees and supervisors, so we rushed past their area every morning to get to our section.

Crossing Paths

Eventually, I bid on a permanent shift from 1:30 PM to 10:30 PM with Thursday's and Friday's off. My friend Alma also had the same schedule. Some of us ladies were scouting out cute men. Alma and I were flirtatious and also single to mingle.

One afternoon, while sitting at my cubicle, I answered a call, "Amtrak Reservations, Yevette speaking, may I help you?" Before the caller could reply my attention was interrupted. As my eyes scanned over the large office space containing approximately two hundred employees, a man suddenly walked through the front door. In the Summer of 1978, *thee one and only* Conrad Jones crossed my path. I will never forget how he made his grand entrance to punch in for his shift.

At the same time, Alma and I looked at each other and said, "Bingo!" This guy was cool as he could be. Just the type of man I was physically attracted to. His overall appearance drew attention. He was a nice-looking man, impeccably dressed in apparel that was not the norm, and his demeanor gave him a presence which demanded attention. Conrad carried himself with such confidence.

In those days, most offices had the big silver time

clocks that hung on the wall accompanied by a set of vanilla timecards with employee's names at the top. You couldn't help but notice who was coming in and getting off their shift because the stamping of the timeclock was extremely loud. Conrad's persona seemed as if he thrived for the moment to walk in that door and turn the heads of onlookers.

Apparently, this good looking brotha' had bid onto my shift. Ironically, Conrad was assigned to sit next to me. "Hello, I'm Conrad Jones and you are?" as he extended his arm for a handshake.
"My name is Yevette, nice to meet you." "Oh, ok Avette," he replied nodding. Conrad talked proper and instead of calling me Yevette he called me

Avette from that day forward. Conrad had a golden-brown complexion, about 6 feet, with a deep voice, slim in stature, excessively well groomed, manicured nails, glowing skin, and texturized hair cut with precision.

He was such a gentleman and pleasure to work alongside that he made the shift go by quicker. Conrad was quite a character with a witty sense of humor and a love for vintage attire. He was so skillfully sharp with his words that he could cut you, and you didn't even know you were bleeding. It dawned on me that his neat presentation somewhat reminded me of my daughter's father that I had fled from.

Our Bond

Early in our friendship I had a crush on Conrad, but as time progressed, I began to have suspicions that he might be gay. He had an animated stroll as if he were on a runway in Paris. As time went by, Conrad and I became good friends. There were times he could make me laugh just by looking at me. He made the craziest faces. We understood one another, we just clicked. Conrad spoke very articulately, was highly intelligent, and he demanded respect.

I admired how he would put the supervisors in their

place when they challenged him or tried to cause a scene. I recall one occasion he said to me, "Oh, they want a scene, baby, I'll give them a scene, they don't want to mess with me Avette." When Conrad finished saying what he had to say, the supervisor was standing there with his jaw dropped lost for words. He did not start conflicts, but he could certainly resolve them with well stated sarcasm.

Conrad and I also had the same days off. Since we spent an eight-hour shift sitting next to each another we shared a lot about ourselves. He loved collecting items from thrift stores that were from the 1940's and 50's era. Conrad's dream was to open a business selling vintage clothing. He planned to name his store, "The Mannequin."

We began to spend our days off hunting for vintage items for his future store. Conrad didn't own a car, so I would pick him up driving from Compton to Baldwin Hills. My house was about twenty minutes away, but the neighborhoods were like night and day. Compton was considered the ghetto. Conrad stayed in a nice community called Baldwin Hills, where most of the residents were African Americans and considered the middle class in that era.

We travelled across the busy streets to Beverly Hills, which is one of the world's most celebrated communities in the heart of Southern

California. This was an upscale area, so the second-hand stores had a better quality of merchandise. The items appeared practically new.

Since around the 1950's Beverly Hills has marketed itself as a high-end shopping paradise featuring Rodeo drive and home of the rich and famous. Millions of visitors flocked to this central location from all over the world every year. Beverly Hills was admired for its lush landscape, near-perfect climate and the exceptional dining, entertainment, shopping, and cultural experiences.

We drove to various places collecting all sorts of things. He showed me all his findings that he accumulated.

Conrad had thousands of vintage pieces for men and women including dresses, antique furniture, beautiful hats, jewelry, and valuable antique artwork. He had so many items that eventually he rented a storage space.

At the time, I was an aspiring model. While working my regular job, I put together my first portfolio. Conrad loaned me most of my outfits for the photo shoot. He had a fabulous collection, which created a beautiful effect for my photos. Conrad was my buddy, and I was so appreciative of his generosity. He really had an eye for fashion.

I will never forget while visiting Conrad one day an unexpected guest rang his doorbell. The way his condo was structured the living room was upstairs, which was divided by a banister. As Conrad went downstairs to answer the door, I leaned over the rail to eavesdrop on his conversation with a male acquaintance. The dialogue that I overheard confirmed my suspicion about his sexuality.

The guy at the door was tall and attractive as well. Conrad was trying to rush him off explaining that his lady friend was visiting. As they parted ways the gentleman leaned in and kissed Conrad on the lips. I silently stepped back out of sight and never asked Conrad about the incident. I figured eventually he would share that personal side of his life, but he never did. In the 1980's, a homosexual lifestyle was not as accepted in society.

At work, Conrad never gave any inkling that he was gay. However, his sexual preference was questionable, yet it was never confirmed. Many Caucasian men on the job were "out of the closet." None of the African American men were making such bold stances. Some employees circulated gossip about Conrad's eccentric style and his failure to mention a female companion.

Oddly, when I met Conrad's mother named Miss Crosby, he casually introduced me as his girlfriend. His mother called him "Butchie" as a nickname. He made it appear as if he was attracted to me, emphasizing how beautiful I was when speaking to his mom.

He also started bringing me around friends outside the job acting as if we were dating. He did it in such a subtle way, he did not feel it necessary to ask me to play along. He just introduced me as his girlfriend Avette. I did not see a reason to address his deception because I knew the truth. He never made any sexual advances toward me, and I realized he needed a cover-up for his secretive lifestyle.

We truly had a special bond, and I considered him to be a real friend. Conrad and I enjoyed going to fashion shows, parties, and disco techs (nightclubs). He taught me how to disco dance. We had so much fun together it was just like hanging out with a brother or a good girlfriend.

    I remember being off the scene for a while parenting and for convenience' sake I decided to take my large purse into the club since it was handy. "Avette where are you going with that big bag?" Conrad asked, laughing. "I need my money and lipstick," I replied. "Nobody carries purses into the club Avette maybe get something small that will go across you." That was so funny to me and when we got inside, we danced the night away like John Travolta.

    I could talk to him about anything, Conrad gave the best advice. If I was upset, he had a way of making me laugh to ease the situation. His genuine concern bought such comfort to any conflict I faced. He loved to make fun of things I wore. I had a pair of wooden clod shoes called Candies that made me feel sassy. "Avette, you got on your come screw me shoes," he joked.

There was an Asian restaurant next door to our job where Conrad and I would sometimes go on our lunch break. It was called Papa Choo's and we loved having an alcohol beverage at the bar. On some occasions, we would drink excessively and would not be able to return to work. We would sneak up into the office and clock ourselves out. We did some of the craziest things at that job.

Conrad taught me some bad work ethics at Amtrak. I recall him getting an irate caller. Conrad said in his serious proper voice, "I am so sorry that you're having that problem sir, hold on, I'm gonna transfer you over to my supervisor Mr. Rel." The man said, "Thank you so much." Little did the man know that Mr. Rel was the "release" button. Once he hung up on the customer, we laughed so hard!

On my days off, after taking my daughter to nursery school I would go straight to pick up Conrad for our vintage shopping excursions. We always laughed at things we observed about people while out in public. We were not rude or obvious to those we focused on, it was more of an inside joke. We had such a goofy and senseless humor. He made the funniest facial expressions, and we would just burst into laughter.

At the time, I was in the dating field, so on some occasions, I would call Conrad for his opinion. He gave great advice on dating as well. We talked on the phone almost every day.

I became romantically involved with another co-worker named Jack. He was the man in my training class that I initially was ignoring. Jack grew on me, and we eventually got married. Conrad was a gifted designer and talented tailor. He volunteered to design my bridesmaid's dresses as a gift to me. I was incredibly happy with the dresses that he made for my special wedding day. They looked amazing. The dresses were pink nylon chiffon that came just below the knee with a sash around the waist.

Conrad along with other co-workers from Amtrak attended our wedding. We had a blast dancing as he shared that memorable day with me. Conrad looked so handsome in his vintage tuxedo. People were also complimenting the delicious food and variety of alcoholic beverages.

Once I became a married woman, my friendship with Conrad was slightly different. I was no longer single and available to spend my "off days" with Conrad. We kept in touch and of course we saw each other at the job. Eventually, to accommodate my duties as a wife I switched my shift to earlier hours.

Our paths hardly ever crossed when I started a new schedule. I also moved to the suburbs thirty minutes outside of Los Angeles. My husband Jack knew Conrad fairly well because we all worked together, so he was not threatened by our friendship. My in-laws were living alternative lifestyles dating the same sex too. Jack was not homophobic since his mom, sister, and son were "out the closet." My life was evolving as I took on new responsibilities in marriage.

Conrad was my voice of reason when I had an argument with my husband. He reminded me of a talk show host and wanted to know both sides before giving any feedback. Conrad was a peace maker and not an instigator.

There were a lot of opposing dynamics in my marriage. I was Jack's third wife, and he had two sets of kids by his two previous wives. Having to deal with both of them calling Jack could be quite overwhelming at times. One of the women was still in love with him and the other had a rude disposition, which was infuriating. Conrad was a safe outlet to vent and express my feelings. My husband never seemed to understand my view on this circle of confusion.

An Invitation

I recall years prior, I got baptized in the titles of the Father, Son, and Holy Ghost at a Baptist church. During that time, I was in pursuit of peace after escaping that abusive relationship with my daughter Nichol's father. However, I did not feel any spiritual transformation afterward. A few weeks later, I regressed back to my old ways. Recreationally, I sniffed lines of cocaine and occasionally smoked marijuana. Also, I tried numbing my pain over the years through alcohol consumption. I grew up believing in God but never established a relationship with Him.

In 1983, I had taken a leave of absence from Amtrak to enroll in cosmetology school. My dad and my child's father Skip both died one month apart. My father died from colon cancer, and Skip was murdered as a result of a drug deal gone bad.

Three months after my father's burial, I picked the phone up and began to dial his number. It hit me like a ton of bricks….. I would never hear his voice again on the other end of my phone. While driving to school, sobbing uncontrollably with my sunroof open, I looked up in the heavens and asked, "Lord how long will I feel this pain?"

When I arrived at Al Tate's Beauty college, I was a little flustered. I took a moment to gather my thoughts before exiting my vehicle since people were used to me being upbeat. It was a busy Saturday morning, and many patrons came to the school to get their hair and nails done. I dried my eyes, put a smile on my face and went in to start my day.

A student at my school that I had become friendly with had some beautiful nail polish on. "Girl, I love that color," I said. "Thanks, my patron over there let me use it, I'm sure she won't mind letting you borrow it," she replied, pointing.

I walked up behind the woman. "Excuse me ma'am may I use your polish?" I asked. She glanced up looking at me in the mirror. "Oh, my goodness **young lady, you** are anointed of the Lord. God is going to save you and then use you to win your entire family to Christ. The Lord told me to tell you, the hurt you feel He is going to heal it!" she adamantly stated.

I stood in amazement that she knew these things. Undoubtedly, this was God. All I heard was her voice. I had blocked out the blow dryers and noisy environment. It seemed like an invisible dome was over just the two of us. That was a pivotal moment that caused the Holy Spirit to begin drawing me. There was a void in my life longing fulfillment.

Shortly after this encounter, a friend named

Barbie got into a fight with another student at the beauty college and was stabbed. I can still remember that chaotic scenario. Barbie dashed passed me in a panic with blood gushing out of her side. She was a Jehovah's Witness trying to convert me, but I had felt quite strongly that wasn't the right path. She was taken off in an ambulance and I did not see her for a while.

Once Barbie recovered, she returned to the beauty college a few months later. She shared a testimony with me about how she had gotten saved according to the scripture Acts 2:38. Barbie was so ecstatic that she joined an Apostolic church and without hesitation I went to visit. At the close of the service, I was pushed down the aisle by what I thought was somebody's hand. I assumed Barbie tried to make a spectacle of me by escorting me to the front. I turned around to say, 'Don't touch me, **I have already** been baptized!' Shockingly, nobody was anywhere around me, and Barbie was still sitting in the pews. I could not say a word after that.

I know what I felt on my back, and right away it dawned on me that the invisible hand of God pushed me to the altar. I heard a whisper, "Eternity is too long to be wrong!" Immediately, I was re-baptized in the name of "Jesus Christ." I felt like a new person! Over the years, people had **emphasized the power of Jesus' name, but** I didn't realize the full significance at the time, but I could tell there was a difference. The Father, Son, and Holy Ghost known as the trinity doesn't implement a name and are nouns/titles. Matthew 28:19, the command was to baptize in the name (singular). After this great day, I tried walking out my faith, but with very little guidance.

Divine Appointment

Once returning to Amtrak from my leave of absence, I was multi-tasking careers. I worked the reservation department during the day and in the evenings, I continued going to beauty college to become a licensed cosmetologist. Conrad and I were glad to see each other as we caught up on the office gossip.

"Avette you won't recognize Sherry Bradshaw when you see her," Conrad said. "Why do you say that is she ill? I asked. "No, she looks fabulous. Sherry lost tons of weight on some kind of diet program she went on," Conrad emphasized. "Oh wow," I replied. Sherry was about four feet-eight inches and quite chubby.

As a newlywed, I gained about ten pounds. Because of my vain temperament, I asked Sherry what her secret was to losing weight. She gave me a business card for a weight loss clinic located in Inglewood, Ca. I made a consultation appointment the same week. I felt so excited about enrolling into this program.

Just so happened, the woman who owned the clinic was a born-again believer. Her name was Ivy, and her assistants name was Jennifer. They began to share the Gospel with me during my first visit to the weight-loss center. I could tell these women were serious about their relationship with the Lord. They attended an Apostolic church, which was the same denomination as Barbie.

Within a few months, I noticed through the scriptures that I still had not completed my salvation. I was lacking the infilling of the Holy Ghost with the evidence of speaking with other tongues (Acts 2:4). According to John 3:5, Mark 16:16-17, and Acts 2:38 the **"water and Spirit" New Birth** is essential.

Initially, I was receptive but after many conversations with Ivy and Jennifer about the Lord, I grew upset. Because of pride, I wanted to believe that they were incorrect. As a child, I was taught that all we had to do was go to church and live a morally upright life to get into heaven. They advised me to, *"Search the scriptures for in them we think we have eternal life* (John 5:39).

One day while driving to the weight loss clinic, I decided to cuss them out if they mentioned another word about receiving the Holy Ghost. All of the sudden, the Lord spoke audibly in a strong tone and said, "Let every man be a lie and let God be true. Whatever she tells you to do, do it!" A vision appeared before me of Ivy sitting at her desk, wearing a white nursing coat, with her hands folded, and the Bible opened on her desk. I was a little shook up. I had only heard God's voice one other time when I was pushed to the altar to get baptized in Jesus' name a few of years prior. Somehow, inwardly I knew this was the voice of God.

When I walked into the clinic, Ivy was literally sitting at her desk just the way I saw her in the vision while driving there. This confirmed that it was truly the Lord. All I could do was throw up my hands.

"Ok I surrender, I'm coming to your church. I want the Holy Ghost," I said, in a desperate tone.

"Hallelujah! I'm so excited. We have Monday Night prayer meeting tonight at 7 PM," Ivy said, as she leaped to her feet with joy.

"Okay, I'm coming right after I leave work."

"You make sure you call me if you start to have any doubt. The enemy does not want you to receive the Holy Ghost," Ivy emphasized.

All day at work, I was excited about the prayer meeting. Then the devil started attacking my mind. I was having second thoughts about meeting Ivy at her church. My Pastor at the Baptist church mocked and warned the congregation about people who spoke in tongues. He taught that the indwelling of the Holy Ghost no longer occurred. Even though I was conflicted, I held on to what the Lord spoke to me earlier that morning.

As I arrived at the church, I was a bit nervous. Satan had me thinking, 'You know your Pastor told you to stay away from those Holiness Churches that believe in speaking in tongues.' I continued anyway and drove onto the property to park in the back. The building was not the typical church structure, so then the devil had me wondering if this was a Kingdom Hall for Jehovah's Witnesses.

I pressed past all those thoughts and went inside. The lights were dim. About twenty-five people were gathered in a circle holding hands as they took prayer requests. I had never been to a Prayer Meeting. A woman introduced herself as Mother Stanley. She was overseeing the prayer gathering.

"Do you have a prayer request?" Mother Stanley asked. Whew! It was my turn. I slowly began to articulate what

I was there for. "I think, I want...the, the Holy Ghost?" I responded, hesitantly. Everyone burst into a jubilant praise! They were shouting, jumping, and rejoicing. The excitement I felt eased the apprehension. I was ready to do whatever it took to get filled with the Holy Ghost.

Mother Stanley took me to the back of the sanctuary to share some scriptures about salvation. Before she could finish reading the verses to me, the anointing engulfed me. "There's no need to continue. You can take me to the altar now!" I expressed. I was kneeling at the altar for about 10 minutes praising God calling on the name of Jesus.

Suddenly, I started speaking in an unknown

language. I was overwhelmed with joy. I began to cry. I stood up, then got back on my knees. I could not believe that God filled me with the gift of the Holy Ghost my first visit to Ivy's church. I asked God to forgive me for doubting him. I left rejoicing. I spoke in tongues the whole forty-five-minute ride home on the freeway.

My life drastically changed. I had no desire to drink and party as I enjoyed doing before. I became a born-again believer in Jesus Christ. I was ecstatic about my conversion that was taking place inwardly and reflecting outwardly. There was such an eagerness to share with everyone. My husband didn't think I was serious because I always ran to church claiming to have gotten saved when my life was in turmoil. I was never the same after this, the power of the Holy Ghost changed everything about me.

Conrad was one of my closest friends, I certainly wanted to share my experience with him. I called him at home. "Oh my God, Conrad I got saved yesterday. I was filled with the Holy Ghost and started speaking in tongues," I said, with amazement. I will never forget what his response was. "Oh Avette, I am so happy for you! You know I speak in tongues too! Ching Chong la la la," Conrad said, in a silly tone.

Conrad, being the comedian that he was, didn't take my encounter with God seriously either. I didn't know what to say in response to his mimicking. He went on to speak in a strange funny language that he made up. I had just got saved and was on a spiritual high from this wonderful experience and felt there was nothing to joke about. It was extremely uncomfortable.

Another day I saw him in the break room at work and began to share with him more about my supernatural encounter and he made fun of me again. His sarcasm was disappointing and his caring personality which he displayed in the past was now fleeting.

Due to my instantaneous deliverance from drinking, our afternoon lunches at Pappa Choo's came to a halt. No more parties, showing out on the dance floor, and I lost interest in modeling High Fashion clothes. I just simply had a new outlook on my life.

That was the beginning of our lives separating. *"How can two walk together except they be agreed"* (Amos 3:3). I was a little sad, but I was determined to walk with God. I often invited Conrad to my church. His response was always the same line, "Avette, I'd love to come, whenever I get a Sunday off."

I passed the State Board exam and received my cosmetology license. Shortly after being born again, I decided to resign from Amtrak. I wanted to go into business for myself as a hairstylist. Conrad and I did not have much in common because of my new Christian lifestyle. It was more like out of sight out of mind after I resigned from Amtrak. I called Conrad occasionally on a holiday or for his birthday. He never kept his promise of visiting my church.

As time went on, I began to embrace the things of God. My life had completely evolved. I pursued God wholeheartedly and became more involved in church activities. There was no turning back for me. Things that I previously found pleasure in had shifted, my friends changed and everything about me.

Me and Conrad's relationship became very awkward. Our conversation was out of sync. His derogatory jokes were no longer humorous. The disco scene was over. The conversations were not as interesting; they were shorter every time we talked. It was obvious we had nothing in common since I had gotten saved.

Due to my immaturity as a babe in Christ, I lacked the wisdom to interact with Conrad without compromising my peace. I didn't know how to continue a friendship without offending him with my biblical beliefs. Ultimately, our interaction dwindled, and our bond grew distant. Our lives were going in opposite directions. Eventually, we lost contact and I was told Conrad moved out of state to Washington DC. I didn't hear from him for a few years after that.

Reunited

About five years later, I received a random phone call from a supervisor at Amtrak. She was a good friend of mine, who knew Conrad was close to me, so she felt compelled to contact me. I could sense by the tone in her voice it was something seriously wrong.

"Yevette, have you talked to Conrad lately?" she asked.

"It's been a while, why what's going on?" I replied, panicking.

"I saw him coming through Amtrak station and he didn't look well at all" she said, somberly.

"Oh, no! I wonder what could be wrong?" I asked.

"I believe he's taken ill Yevette, I think you need to call him."
"Thank you so much for calling to inform me," I said.

At that very moment, a strange feeling came over me, and I thought, 'Oh my God! What about Conrad?' I knew my friend had pure intentions by notifying me. Immediately, I called to reconnect with Conrad. He was living with his Mother Miss Crosby in Washington, D.C. One thing I know about true friendship, no matter what you go through in life you will be there for one another.

The phone rang a few times and he answered. "Ohhh, Avette," he said. His voice sounded so needy, so serious. There were a few seconds of silence.

"Hey, what's going on, how are you doing?" I asked.

"Not too good Avette. I have something to tell you," Conrad said in a sad tone.

"What is it, Conrad?" I asked, concerned.

"I am dealing with a sickness that has no cure. I'm not expected to live long at all," he said.

"What kind of sickness?" I asked, hesitantly.

"Avette, I have contracted AIDS."

I was speechless for a few seconds.

"Oh no Conrad! Wow, um, I'm so sorry."

    I didn't know what else to say. I had to gather my thoughts. My heart was hurt. Once I processed this devastating news, I realized that my friend Conrad was terminally ill. I expressed my love and said a prayer with him. After I hung up the phone I sat there in disbelief.

In the late 80's and early 90's there wasn't a lot of information about HIV/AIDS. There were just experimental drugs being prescribed. I didn't really know much about the virus myself. In that era, many employees at Amtrak had already died from AIDS.

My mind and emotions were all over the place. I thought to myself, 'Why didn't he come to church when I invited him? Now he's all the way in Washington, DC. Oh My God! His soul is going to spend eternity somewhere.' I began to intercede through prayer and ask God to save my friend. I needed a plan. I felt an urgency to go visit Conrad.

Faith Flight

Eventually, I called my friend Jennifer. Her husband Josh worked for the airlines. I explained to Jennifer that my good friend Conrad was extremely sick, and I wanted to go see him because he wasn't saved. She checked with her husband Josh to see if he had a "buddy pass," which allowed friends or family to fly for free.

I asked my husband Jack if he was okay with me going out of town for a few days. My daughter was in high school, so Nichol could practically take care of herself. Jack agreed that I should go minister to Conrad. It was a relief to have my husband on board. 'Thank you, Jesus!' I thought, as I packed my suitcase.

Before I left Los Angeles, I gathered with my prayer warriors Sister Ivy, Sister Jennifer, and Sister Maggie. We were all members of the same church in California and were good friends. We often met at Ivy's weight loss clinic to pray, have bible study, and corporately fast together for a spiritual breakthrough. The four of us had a burden for evangelism and wanted to urge souls to obey the Acts 2:38 plan of salvation. Our faith fueled us with anticipation of the imminent return of the Lord.

"For the LORD himself will come down from heaven, with

a loud command, with the voice of the archangel and with the trumpet call of God, and the dead in Christ will rise first. After that, we who are still alive and are left will be caught up together with them in the clouds to meet the LORD in the air. And so, we will be with the LORD forever" (1 Thessalonians 4:16-17).

March 1992, I was solely focused on making a trip to Washington D.C. to visit Conrad. Somehow, I believed the way would be made for him to be baptized in Jesus' name and filled with the Holy Ghost. I had no idea how it was going to happen, but I believed God. Off to Washington I went on a missionary journey!

The Plan

When I arrived in Washington, D.C., I took a cab to Conrad's house where he lived with his mother. I did not know what to expect as I walked by faith. God sent me on this assignment and one thing I realized, is that I had limited time. My main objective and fervent prayer was to find a church that would baptize my friend in the name of Jesus and also that Conrad would be filled with the Holy Ghost (Acts 2:4, Acts 2:38).

Once I arrived, his mother Miss Crosby gave me a big hug. She introduced me to their cousin Sheila who was also visiting from California. Then, Miss Crosby escorted me down the hall to Conrad's room. When I entered, he was sitting up in his bed awaiting me like an excited kid at Christmas. There were tubes coming out of various parts of his body, which were connected to some sort of machine. Conrad had a full-time nurse on staff during the day. His health seemed to be declining rapidly.

He had on a pair of red and black checkered pajamas. Conrad's hair had fallen out and grown back with a beautiful curly texture. He was well groomed as only Conrad would be under the circumstances. He was neat, clean, glowing, and every hair was in place. He looked at me with those big brown eyes full of tears and had a tender boy like look on his face. "Ohhh, Avette, look what I've done to myself, He said, ashamed. "Oh Conrad," I responded, tenderly.

As I sat on the side of his bed, I hugged him so tight. We had a moment of silence. God gave me strength to keep my composure. I had to stay spiritually focused.

I had not been there but a few hours when his mother entered to ask, "Hey Butchie, (that was his nickname from his mom) I'm about to walk to the market, do you want anything? "
"No, I don't mom," he replied.

I decided to walk with her to get out and see a little bit of Washington, D.C. since it was my first time there. In March, the snow was freshly melted, so it was still cold. It took us about an hour or so round-trip. We walked to the store but on the way back she hailed a Gypsy taxi. Being from California I had never heard of a Gypsy taxi. In today's world it would be considered an Uber service. The first day, I was spying out the land like Joshua and Caleb in Numbers 13.

Due to my limited stay, immediately I started searching the Yellow Pages to find a listing of an Apostolic or Pentecostal church in the city. I called several places to ask if they could pick Conrad up to baptize him. I had given it no thought how he would be able to leave the house hooked up to that machine. Conrad was fading slowly. At that time, people were very afraid of interaction with someone who contracted AIDS because they were not educated.

The only thing on my mind was Conrad's soul. I didn't expect a church to turn anyone down, especially for someone whose life was on the line. Once I explained that he was on his deathbed all of them replied, "I'll call you back."

Sadly, no one ever responded. I was only visiting Washington, D.C. for three days. The hours were counting down, and I was determined. My total dependency was on God. This was the first occasion I had experienced anything like this, which caused me to be a little nervous.

Conrad and I were in his room reminiscing about our history at Amtrak. We talked about the "old times" when we hunted for vintage clothing on our days off, attending fashion shows, and how he taught me to disco tech. We even cracked up with laughter reflecting on the occasion we got intoxicated on our lunch break and couldn't go back to work. Though Conrad was a little frail, my presence made him happy and lifted his spirit.

The second day I was there, his mother was making another trip to the store. She asked me if I wanted to go with her, but I declined. I decided to stay with Conrad. It was beginning to seem like the movie, "Mission Impossible." I'd come too far to abort the assignment.

I sought wise counsel over the phone with my three prayer warriors in Los Angeles. Sister Ivy and Sister Jennifer were both nurses. Sister Ivy was giving me strategy, which she attained many spiritual gifts (1 Cor. 12:7-11). God dealt with Sister Maggie in visions, so she had spiritual insight also. I gave them step by step detailed updates of what was going on. Back then in the 90's most people didn't have cell phones, so I was using the landline.

I was praying with Conrad, reading the Bible to him, and trying to persuade him to get saved. At that point, it wasn't much resistance from him at all. If God didn't work a miracle, he was on his way into eternity without his name written in the Lamb's Book of Life.

God's Grace

The day before, I had already accompanied Conrad's mother to the store, so I knew the estimated turn around. All the years I had known her, she never talked about religion. Now, Conrad reveals that his mom is a devout Catholic. He also emphasized that she would not agree with anything outside of her beliefs. I would have never guessed this in a million years.

I followed the leading of the Lord to move swiftly in his mother's absence. I had less than an hour before Miss Crosby would return. My adrenaline was pumping. I called Sister Ivy and Jennifer for prayer. Sister Maggie spoke a prophetic word, which was a confirmation to forge ahead. The Holy Spirit prompted me to baptize Conrad myself.

Little did I know, the Lord had already orchestrated these plans. Conrad's cousin Sheila from California was a registered nurse. He also had a private LVN that came daily. God always has a ram in the bush!

I asked Sheila and his private nurse to assist me. I needed their help since he was hooked up to a machine connected through tubes. Fortunately, Conrad's cousin was a Christian, so she was on board with the idea right away.

It was apparent how ill Conrad was because the LVN was on duty 12 hours every day. The Lord pricked his heart to get baptized in the name of Jesus Christ for the remission of his sins (Acts 2:38, Mark 16:16-17, 1 Peter 3:21). What a mighty God we serve!

Anyone with a spiritual background would have wanted to help Conrad prepare to meet Jesus for eternity. Since they were both nurses it was a blessing from a medical standpoint. What was even more amazing, Conrad's mother had a round Jacuzzi style bathtub. How awesome is that?

The nurses detached Conrad from the machine and wrapped the tubes with plastic. Surprisingly, the tub was a perfect fit. God is the master planner; he was really blowing my mind! In that short hour or so we had enough time to prepare the water.

My prayer warriors at home were instructing me every step of the way over the phone. Sister Ivy suggested that I put some kitchen gloves on to cover any fresh burns on my arms from pressing hair. The virus was such a mystery, we didn't know how it was transmitted, so I wanted to take proper precautions. The two nurses put Conrad over in the tub.

"Conrad, pray aloud and ask God to forgive you of all your sins," I said.

"God please forgive me for not serving you and surrendering my life sooner, but I genuinely want to see you in peace.

Cleanse me of my sins in Jesus name," Conrad prayed.

For years, I worked with baptism candidates at my church, so I knew the formula to recite. "My dearly beloved, Conrad Jones upon the confession of your faith and the blessed confidence we have in the written word of God concerning our Lord and Savior Jesus Christ; His death, His burial, and His resurrection, I do indeed take pleasure in baptizing you into the name of our Lord and Saviour Jesus Christ for the remission of all your sins and you shall receive the gift of the Holy Ghost!"

I fully immersed Conrad gently under the water calling the name of Jesus Christ over him. Hallelujah! Hallelujah! I was excited and so was he. It seemed like his countenance lit up when he came up out of the water in the newness of life putting on Christ (Romans 6:3-4, Galatians 3:27).

We had to move quickly to get him redressed while watching the clock. Miss Crosby could come home at any given moment. Being that she did not have a car and had to walk or take a taxi it was about forty minutes until she would return. God was moving all the while!

We all rejoiced, clapping, and leaping. Conrad's cousin Sheila and his nurse hurried to get him dressed and dry out the jacuzzi tub, so that everything looked the same. As they tucked Conrad back into bed, I asked if he wanted to receive the Holy Ghost?

"Yes!" he replied, with excitement.

"Luke 11:13 says, 'The Holy Spirit is given to anyone who asks,'" I replied.

"Fill me Lord," he said.

"Just start praising God Conrad. As an expression of praise, repeatedly say aloud, 'Thank you Jesus.' You are thanking him in advance for the Holy Ghost. It may feel like you are getting tongue-tied but don't assume it's because you are repeating yourself; this is the sign that God is trying to transition you into your prayer language. Speak out the unknown sounds and the stuttering will get clearer as you talk out those syllables," I instructed.

One thing I know, it does not take God a long time to do anything. In a matter of moments Conrad was speaking with other tongues. He was so joyous! He looked at me with tears streaming down his face.

"Oh, my friend, my friend Avette, you came to save me."

"I didn't save you Conrad the Lord saved you, He just sent me here as an Apostolic Missionary," I said.

God truly completed this whole process quickly. What an awesome God we serve! His cousin Sheila and his nurse on duty were in awe as they celebrated. I was ecstatic! All of us were rejoicing with Conrad as though we had been acquainted for years. I just met his cousin and the nurse on the previous day. At that very moment, there was an instant bond between us that was indescribable. We were like little children withholding a secret from mommy.

Conrad was a grown, forty something year old man. In the midst of all that rejoicing he beckoned me to his bedside to warn me. "Avette, you better not tell my mother that you baptized me because she would be terribly angry," Conrad said, paranoid. The devil sure can bring a spirit of fear upon people. It was too late now; Conrad was Bible saved according to Acts 2:38. His mother's Catholic beliefs were irrelevant, but I honored my friend's wishes to use discretion.

Miss Crosby returned from the store within fifteen minutes of this miraculous move of God. Their cousin Sheila, his nurse, and I were sitting in the living room looking suspicious. We were about to burst with excitement holding this secret. Sheila even knew it was not a good idea to tell Miss Crosby about what took place while she was at the store.

There was a silence in the room as if we were holding our breath. Miss Crosby sensed there was something going on. "What have you all been doing? How is Butchie?" she asked. "He's fine," we all responded in unison like a choir. We were fidgeting around, looking back and forth at one another. Finally, the nurse suggested that we all go outside and get some fresh air. We put our coats on and rushed out the house quickly, so that we could discuss this phenomenon.

We walked down the street and immediately praised God! As we walked a few blocks from the apartment complex, the nurse pointed over to a little church across the street. "That's the church I was raised in," she said. I looked over at the church. The sign read "Apostolic."

Oh my God! This was ironic. Conrad's nurse was the same denomination as me, Apostolic (Pentecostal). She went on to explain that she was a backslider, which means a believer who had fallen away from her faith. The nurse emphasized the importance of water baptism in the name of Jesus Christ, which caused her to jeopardize her job. I was speechlessly amazed. Then, Conrad's cousin Sheila confessed that she was filled with the Holy Ghost speaking in tongues too and had not been vocal about it because most of her family was Catholic.

We rejoiced even more, right there on the sidewalk sharing that wonderful moment together hugging and crying in amazement. Here we were, three strangers who God brought together for "Such a time as this." I will never forget that moment for the rest of my life. God answered a prayer that seemed insurmountable and heard my concerns, "What about Conrad?"

"The things which are impossible with men are possible with God." Luke 18:27

The next day, I looked in the Yellow Pages directory to find a Christian bookstore. I took a taxicab to buy Conrad a baptism certificate. I flew there with my brand-new Ryrie Study Bible and decided to give it to him also. I wanted Conrad's experience to be special, so I signed the Bible and wrote a letter to him about his New Birth experience.

Sworn to secrecy, my mission was accomplished. It was time for me to go home. My God had done exceedingly abundantly above all I could ask or think (Ephesians 3:20). I said goodbye to my dear friend and made preparation to go home.

Unspoken Confession

Once I returned to Los Angeles, Conrad and I remained in contact. He was so enthusiastic about being baptized in the name of Jesus and receiving the gift of the Holy Ghost. I often encouraged him. We prayed together weekly and shared scriptures over the phone. I was at peace with his fate. Whatever happened now, God had answered my prayer and Conrad was "saved."

One morning, I was trying to get out the door to a funeral for a deacon at my church and the phone rang. It was Conrad and he was noticeably short of breath, and barely able to get his words out. The sickness had taken a toll on him. I was preoccupied putting on my shoes in a hurry. He was trying to gather his words. I didn't want to be late, and my destination was a forty-five-minute commute.

"Hey Conrad! I'm just walking out the door, what's going on?"
"I have something to tell you, Avette," he said, gasping.
"Okay, can I call you when I return home? I'm on my way to a funeral service for a member of my church," I explained.
"Sure, don't forget Avette bye," Conrad said, in a whisper.

    I felt it would be better for us to talk later and we would have more time to share. When I came home, it was a little later than I had anticipated. I figured he would be asleep, so I decided to call him in the morning. The next call I received was from his mother, Miss Crosby.

"Hello, Yvette, this is Miss Crosby, she said.

"Hi Miss Crosby, how are you?"

"Not too good, I was calling to let you know that Butchie passed away," she said.

"Aww, I'm sorry my condolences and prayers. Let me know when his funeral will be. I appreciate you calling," I said, affectionately.

Butchie was her nickname for Conrad. I surely did not think yesterday would be the last conversation I had with my friend. I took a deep breath. My heart sunk. Though I knew this day would come, I was hopeful for a miracle that God might heal him. It was three months and 11 days after our visit together in Washington, D.C. My friend Conrad passed away and went home to be with the Lord on July 12, 1992.

What About Conrad

There was a co-worker from Amtrak named George who contacted me about Conrad's passing. He was so sad because they were good friends as they worked together all those years. I began to share the miraculous testimony about Conrad's salvation on his deathbed.

George was planning to attend the funeral services too. "George, don't you want to get saved. Life is so short. We all must obey Acts 2:38. I strongly suggest before you board that red-eye flight please meet me at my church tonight and get baptized in the name of Jesus

Christ," I said, passionately. "Yes, I have avoided God my entire life. I will come to your church what's the address?" he asked.

"1003 south Prairie Avenue in Inglewood just 5 minutes from the airport, so bring your luggage," I said.

My church, Peace Apostolic would open even if there was no service scheduled. They baptized 7 days a week if someone desired to be saved. I called to arrange the baptism for that evening. I lived almost an hour away, but I didn't mind driving because I was eager about souls. I prayed in my heavenly language in route to the church.

George met us at the church promptly. My Pastor,

Bishop Howard Swancy baptized him personally. The church secretary and I took George to the altar to kneel on the padded benches. Within thirty minutes of praising God, he was speaking in tongues. Another victorious outcome! George left for the airport rejoicing born again of the water and Spirit.

I flew back to Washington D.C. the following day for the funeral. There was just a few of us from Los Angeles that attended his service. Conrad didn't have very many relatives or friends that lived in the D.C. area. It was a small, quaint, and extremely sweet memorial gathering. When the service was over, we all ended up back at his mother's house. Towards the end of the evening, I approached Miss Crosby.

"Would you mind if I took back the Bible I had given Conrad when I was here a few months ago?" I asked.

"No, not at all Yevette," she replied.

    I walked down the hallway to Conrad's room and retrieved the Bible beside his bed. I was able to return home with the cherished memory of being instrumental in his salvation that afternoon in March. It was bittersweet. I knew I would not see Conrad again in this life, nor hear his voice on the other end of the phone. However, it was comforting knowing that he was in the arms of Jesus for eternity.

This was the note written in the Bible to my dearest friend dated April 1, 1992. Conrad, you have now completed your salvation according to the word of God. The scriptures are all we must go by. Remember, there's only one way to enter the kingdom of God. You have found that one way! Thank you Jesus! No one gets the credit but Jesus alone! Always pray and ask God to open your understanding before you read. Don't let any man deceive you about the word of God. Always go to the word of God on your own. Remember, God will always give you a confirmation in his word about any questions you may have. If someone gives you a prophecy and they say it is from God, tell them to show it to you in the word. If they have

no scripture to back it up don't receive it. Stand on the word. Remember the scripture I gave you. St. John 1:1 In the beginning was the Word and the Word was with God, and the Word was God. Love you always!
Sincerely, Yevette

Shortly after Conrad 's death, his mother moved back to Los Angeles. Miss Crosby wasn't far from where I was living. I decided to go visit her one evening. Surprisingly, she had been drinking and was a little tipsy. I didn't know this side of her, so I felt a tad bit uneasy.

Just before I got ready to leave, Miss Crosby stood up and pointed at me. By this time, she had consumed several drinks. "You think I don't know what you did Yevette?" she asked, in a stern tone. She appeared to be a little offended.

"I don't know what you're talking about Miss Crosby," I responded, in suspense.

"Butchie told me that you baptized him when you were at our house," she said, angry.

"I cannot believe that you are upset about your "terminally ill" son deciding to secure his eternal resting place," I replied.

    While Miss Crosby attempted to give a rebuttal, her slurred speech and body language became aggressive, so it was apparent that this visit was over. I slowly began to gather my belongings. As I walked toward the door, I spoke my final words. "Conrad asked me to keep it confidential, but I am glad that you are aware of it. I beseech you to obey Acts 2:38, just like your son did. Repent, turn from your sins and be baptized in the name of Jesus Christ and filled with the gift of the Holy Ghost if you expect to see Conrad again Miss Crosby," I said, in a preaching tone as I closed the door behind me.

I always wondered if the "unspoken confession" before he passed away was about his mom knowing he got saved. He couldn't get the words out of his mouth as he gasped for air during our last conversation. For years, that subtly disturbed me because I wish I knew what he was going to tell me.

I never spoke with Miss Crosby again. I received a phone call from her cousin

Sheila shortly after she became irate during my visit.

"Hi Yevette, I wanted to tell you Conrad's mom was found in her apartment unresponsive from an aneurysm," Sheila said.

"Oh, wow I'm sorry to hear that," I replied, concerned.

"Yeah, she never recovered. She was put into a low-income nursing facility in a run-down area," Sheila added.

"How awful, I appreciate you letting me know I will be praying for Miss Crosby," I replied.

I was glad Conrad's cousin Sheila had touched base to inform me. Out of my love for Conrad I went to the facility to see Miss Crosby, but she was in a vegetated state. She had no idea who I was. I was in disbelief and instantly thought how Conrad would have been heartbroken to see his mother sitting in a place such as that. She was in one of those cotton hospital gowns they put on everyone. Miss Crosby was sitting in a wheelchair drooling with her head slumped over.

Unfortunately, she did not take heed to the words I gave her concerning making her calling and election sure (2 Peter 1:10). Miss Crosby died shortly after I saw her at the nursing home. Not many people have an opportunity to get saved on their deathbed such as Conrad. *"The day you hear his voice harden not your heart"* Hebrews 3:15.

Obey Acts 2:38 before it's everlasting too late!

www.ingramcontent.com/pod-product-compliance
Lightning Source LLC
LaVergne TN
LVHW021404080426
835508LV00020B/2445